BELIEVE FROM WITHIN

How **Basketball** Changed My Life

To: Teresa

#21

Lee Green

A Book by

Lee **Green**

D1158540

CONTENTS

ACKNOWLEDGEMENTS

As I have encountered so many great people who have played an intricate part of my life. I want to first begin by thanking my Lord and Savior Jesus Christ for his unconditional love. I have been through the highs and lows of life and without my Lord and Savior I wouldn't have been able to get through the challenges and difficulties that are part of life. Even when I wasn't acknowledging him my Lord Savior was still there protecting me.

Also with what I have been able to accomplish thus far in my life; such as playing Division 1 basketball, building a successful business with zero business experience, getting married, buying my first home and vehicle and as he continues to give me the opportunity to impact the lives of so many different individuals in such a positive manner, it wouldn't have been possible without his grace and mercy.

I would like to also thank my mother (Beverly Jackson) for her many sacrifices that position me to be successful in the classroom, on the court and beyond the game of basketball. I would like to thank my beautiful wife (Nichole Green) for being by side through the highs and lows. Beside every successful man is a strong and supportive woman. I want to thank my three kids (Jeremiah Green, Destanie Green and Trinitee Green) for their unconditional love and their daily inspiration.

I would like to also thank (Mrs. Loretta McFrarland) for speaking in my life when I was at a crossroads. The day you invited me to church my life has never been the same. Thank you for taking the time to pour into my life when I needed it the most. I would also like to thank my mentor Archbishop E. Bernard Jordan for helping me expand my business to new levels and for bringing out the gift of prophecy out of my life. Your wisdom has made a tremendous impact in my life through my business, marriage and many other areas. Thank you, Archbishop E. Bernard Jordan, for taking the time to speak life into me.

Thanks to the many coaches who have helped me along the journey, Bob Kirk, Bucky Lee, Cokey Roberston, Todd Rideout, Alvin Brooks, Fred Rike, and Johnny Jones without all of you I would not been the man that I am. I would like to thank all the parents who have allowed their children to join the Lee Green Basketball organization. I appreciate all of you because of you

I have been able to continue to fulfill my God give purpose in hopes of helping the youth succeed beyond the game of basketball.

I also would like to thank the the coaches who continue to actively support the Lee Green Basketball vision. Thank you, James Briscoe, Renata Goeins, Angie Naurez, Irin Pruitt, Avery Carey, Alicia Myers, Todd Rideout, Mike Gunn, Susie Evans, Tina Strelke, Eric McCarty and Troy Dunn. I would like to thank you all for what you have done for the kids who are enrolled in the Lee Green Basketball organization.

Thanks also to Emily Metzloff (proofreader) thank you for your consistent effort that you put towards in helping me complete my first of many books to come. I would like to thank John Sternig (designer) thank you for your patience and feedback.

I'm blessed to have had great memories with all of those who have had such a positive impact on my life. These experiences have allowed me to share my story through my first book and I'm so grateful for all of you.

Much Gratitude,

Lee Green

INTRODUCTION

It's Been Birthed

This book was originally supposed to have been written years ago. However, I didn't fully commit to writing this book until now. And now, finally, my first book has been birthed. There were many people telling me that I should write a book. Some of those people had heard me give inspirational talks to kids, watched one of my inspirational videos on social media, or they just know my journey and believe that sharing my story and wisdom could benefit others.

I have a passion for helping others discover their purpose and succeed. Seeing others succeed brings joy to my heart, as I know each of us have been put on this earth with a purpose that no one else can fulfill but us.

As I write this book, there has been a lot of brutally, crime, and terrorism happening in our country. However, I believe this is not the time to be in fear. However, it is the time for us to make a positive imprint on others through our God-given purpose.

Discovering your purpose and becoming clear on what it is that brings you fulfillment is the beginning of you living a life that brings complete satisfaction.

Therefore, I knew that this was the perfect time to write this book and to share my story in hopes of inspiring others. There have been many people who have played a part in bringing this book to fruition both indirectly and directly, whether it was coach taking me to practice when I didn't have a ride or my mom taking me to her job and showing me wwhat manual labor looks like or a mentor coming into my life to help me fulfill my life's purpose.

However, this book is more than me sharing my life journey with you. This book is about showing you how God took a young boy like me, raised by a single parent who worked 12 hour days, who sacrificed to put clothes on my back and my sibling's backs and who showed me what hard work really looked like through her actions. This book is designed to inspire, uplift and to encourage you to step outside of your comfort zone and do something that's bigger than you so others who you come in contat with can gain of hope and clarity by you pursuing your life's purpose.

We all go through the ups and downs of life, whether it's losing a love one or sibling like I have or losing a job you dedicated your life to for over 20+ years. At some level, we have all dealt with pain, adversity, and/or setbacks in our life. However, this book will encourage you to get back up and keep fighting the good fight of faith. Just like the Bible scripture reads in Mark 9:23 "...*anything is possible if a person believes.*"

My hope is that after reading this book you will be inspired to do something that is positive and bigger than you, so others may be inspired by your story. Or just maybe after reading this book you will have gained discovered your life's purpose. As Russell Simmons says in his book Do You! "*Success is a journey, not a destination.*"

I want to thank you for allowing me to share my failures, success, and wisdom with you.

Where it all started

At the age of seven years old, my mother began to introduce me to sports. Since that age, sports have been an intricate part of my life. The first sport that I was introduced to, ironically, was baseball. I began playing tee-ball at seven years old, which didn't last very long. I remember going out to a tryout for the first time. After the coaches watched me hit the ball off the tee a few times and catch a couple ground balls, the coaches walked over to my mother and told her that I didn't belong in tee-ball and that I should be in little league. However, there was one problem: the little league baseball league was for kids between the ages of 9 to 12 years old. However, my mother gave them the okay to move me up, and this is where it all began.

There will be times where you will need the assistance of others to push you towards your destiny. My mom had no ability of what my ability was when it came to baseball. She never saw me play the sport; all she recalls is getting me a pitching machine to help me improve my hitting. What she may not have realized at that time was that God was using her to plant the seed. Her signing me up for tryouts gave me the opportunity to be exposed

11

to coaches who had a general understanding of the game and the passion to teach the game.

It's amazing how one person can plant the seed, then another will water it, and then God will give the increase? For me this has always been my life experience. As I began to excel in baseball between 8 and 12 years old, my mom decided to get me into football at the age of 10. However, I really enjoyed playing baseball for one reason, and it wasn't because I enjoyed playing in the 90-degree weather! I enjoyed it because I felt as though I had a sense of control of the outcome, especially when I was pitching or hitting, at least I thought I was in control.

As I began to transition to playing football, I quickly realized the different dynamic between baseball and football. Football taught me at an early age how to embrace contact. Though I was tall for an average 10 year old, I was skinny and only weighed about 100 pounds and competing against guys that were much bigger than me and weighed 100 pounds more than me. But I quickly began to have success as a running back, rushing for 100+ yards per game and scoring multiple touchdowns in each game. Football quickly became one my favorite sports to play.

I went on to play baseball and football up until my 8th grade year, and that's when I decided to choose another sport. One of the reasons I chose a different sport was because I was already thinking about my professional career at 12 years old. Yes, my mom would tell you I had goals written out about playing professionally. I would put them on my wall in my bedroom, hang them from my mom's rearview mirror in her car, and I would carry them with me in my wallet.

At 12 years old, I was already thinking about which sport would give me the shortest path to the professional ranks. I knew I was way too small in stature to compete at a high level in football, though some would say I had the foot speed, agility and instincts to do it. However, I just knew in my heart that football wasn't it. Then I looked at baseball. I thought about the different ranks that you had to go through to get to the MLB: Single A, Double A, Triple A and then the majors. I felt that process would take too long and my chances were too slim. Also, I knew baseball was a technical sport and I never had any professional training. Though I was a good hitter, infielder, outfielder and pitcher, most of that came from my God-given athleticism and instincts, and the rest came from hard work.

So, then I was introduced to basketball at 12 years old. I was so behind fundamentally with basketball they put me in the Pee-Wee league. You know, the league where beginners play. I felt so embarrassed because I knew how good I was in other sports, but with basketball, things weren't clicking as easily. Therefore, being the competitor that I am, I began to go to the local park by myself and work on my game. It was to the point that I was doing dribbling moves down the sidewalk every night around 8 or 9 pm, and remember this lady would always come out of her house just to tell me to stop dribbling the ball. I just fell in love with the game, and what really triggered that love was the challenge that I had to overcome with my lack of fundamentals. See my peers were very good when it came to basketball, as most of them had been playing since they were 8 years old like I had been with baseball. But I took that as a challenge. I said to myself, I will one day be better than them.

The one thing that I quickly learned about basketball unlike the other sports was the fact that you really didn't need anyone there to help. I mean it would have been good to have someone rebounding my shots, but besides that, I loved the fact that I could focus on the skills that I needed to improve by myself.

There will be times in your life that you just must have that secret place so you can perfect the necessary skills you need to excel in the arena that you're in.

See with baseball, to improve your pitching, you need someone to catch your pitches. And with football, to improve your catching skills, you need someone to pass the ball to you.

I believe if there had been an opportunity to work with a professional one on one, my mother without doubt would have made the sacrifice to get me professional training. However, in the community that I grew up in, that was unheard of. As a kid, I was always under the impression that you had to do it yourself. I had no idea that you could get a professional trainer if you had the means to do so. I pretty much had to grow up without my dad around, so I didn't have anyone to work with me and show me the way. I had to pretty much teach myself, which I had no problem doing, as I saw it as a challenge.

Way too often, people when faced with a challenge or obstacle make excuses, and I could have been one of them. I remember going from the Pee-Wee league to entering the Junior basketball league, which is the more competitive league. And I just happened to be the first pick of that season. And sure enough, I was drafted to the weakest team. The first year, our team didn't do too well. We ended up finishing in last place in the league. Our team was pretty much the laughing stock of the league. However, I did make the all-star team, which gave me a boost of confidence, but I still had a lot of improving to do. And I was willing to continue to put in the work at the level that I needed to be at. The following year I was asked to play on a traveling team. This was the team that the best players in the city were selected to play on. This was a game changer for me. The passion to succeed, the commitment to put in the work was there, but I just needed the extra push to get to the level that I desired to be. And then enter a coach by the name of Todd Rideout, who began to teach me the fundamentals that I needed to elevate my game to get to the next level.

As you get deeper into these chapters, I am going to share with you some of my success principles, and one of them has to do with having a mentor and/or coach. Everyone needs a coach in their life, and I'm not just speaking in terms of playing a sport. A coach is someone who can see your blind spots, as one of my mentors who I will discuss later, always said to me.

After playing travel basketball, which prepared me for my second year of junior league basketball, we ended up with the first draft pick. And we drafted a neighborhood friend of mine who was also a talented athlete by the name of Marcus Chung. You want to talk about being blessed with natural quickness, he was the one. Drafting him made my job a lot easier. Teams could no longer key on me with double teams; they now had another player to worry about. That season we went on to become the regular season champs and tournament champs.

With just two years of experience playing organized basketball, my mom was approached by a couple of individuals about the opportunity to play basketball at a prestigious private school called St. Maria Goretti, a school that was well known for producing some good basketball players, some of whom went on to play in college and the NBA. The only problem was that it cost a good amount of money for my mother to send me to this school and it wasn't like we had the funds to do it.

I recall times where we had to sleep fully clothed because my mom was unable to pay for gas and electricity during that time. Deep down, I knew my mom was doing the best that she could to make sure that all of our needs were being taken care of. I knew as a single mother of three kids that it was challenging to provide for us and maintain a roof over our head.

Experiences like this taught me how to appreciate the things that she could buy me and it taught me that my value was not in the name brand clothes and the shoes that I wore. Though we all desire nice things, it's important to keep a proper perspective. My mother pondered the thought of sending me to this private school. Both her and I knew that it would be a sacrifice financially for me to go there. However, my mom was willing to make the sacrifices needed for me to attend St. Maria Goretti. And I'm so glad that she did.

> There will be times in your life where you must go beyond your circumstances to create the opportunity that you so desire.

There will be times in your life where you must go beyond your circumstances to create the opportunity that you so desire. I personally believe my mom had a clear image of my future and the significant role St. Maria Goretti would play in it or else she would've never made the move to send me to Goretti given our circumstances. Whether, it was the amount of money that she did or did not have in the bank account or the number of bills that she had.

The reality is many of us continue to miss out on opportunities due to the failure to see beyond our current circumstances. It's the mental image that you hold in your mind regarding the future that will push you to your destiny. See, most of us have an image of negativity and failure, where we should have an image of positivity and possibility.

The summer before my freshman year of high school, my travel coach Todd Rideout decided to take me to the inner city of Baltimore to play for Coach Bucky Lee and the Oliver Owls. When I say, this experience took my basketball skills and determination to another level, I mean it. Coach Bucky was one of those coaches that didn't play any games. He would get in your face and call you out, especially if he felt as though you weren't pushing hard

> As we move in the direction of our dreams and goals, it's important that we remain coachable.

enough or playing at the level that he expected you to play at. For him it was about finding a way to get the best out of you both mentally and physically.

He knew I was committed to putting in the hard work and he also knew I struggle with the mental aspect of the game. It was a challenge for me to accept when coaches would hold me accountable. Most of it came from me being immature and some of it had to do with my father who wasn't consistently present in my life as a young kid. It was my mother's voice that I consistently heard when it would result in me being disciplined.

As we move in the direction of our dreams and goals, it's important that we remain coachable. Those who are willing to learn and be held accountable will succeed under any circumstances. Those who aren't coachable will be the ones who will remain stagnant and ultimately push away those who sincerely want to help them succeed.

I recall one of the first practices that I had with my AAU Coach Bucky Lee. I vividly remember a situation where he felt as though I wasn't practicing up to his standard. And, he immeately yelled at me and told me to step up my game or get out of his gym. He went on a tirade for a couple minutes just scolding me I looked at my mother, and I said "I quit I want nothing to do with this anymore." And my mom looked right at me and said "Son you're not going anywhere, get back on the court." She understood that this situation was good for me, especially being a young man who was growing up without a father in his life. I believe that she knew that this was the right time of my life where I needed someone other than her to hold me accountable. After Coach Bucky yelled at me and challenged me to go harder in front of everybody in the gym, my mother could have easily taken me out of the situation, and she would have had every right to do so. The way he got on to me most parents today would have step in and pull their child off the court immediately and would have returned to the team.

But my mother understood what the coach was trying to do for me and it was exactly what I needed at that time. Coach Bucky was a great coach who challenged me in a way that brought the best out of me. My skills and mental toughness would go to greater levels after a few summer AAU seasons with Coach Bucky.

If you are parent who has a child or children who are athletes my suggestion to you is to look for coaches who have your child's best interest whe it comes to their success both on and off the court. The coaches who I had great success under on and off the court did exactly that. They truly cared about my success off the court as much as they did on the court and that's what great coaches do.

How often do we run from situations that don't seem to conform to what we want at that moment of time? Running from the situation is failing to face the situation head on. Oftentimes we embellish the situation, which leads to us making emotional decisions. I once heard someone say to me, when your emotions are high, your intelligence is low. We should avoid making crucial decisions when our emotions are high.

> I once heard someone say to me, when your emotions are high, your intelligence is low.

I thank my mother to this day for not taking me off the court and allowing me to quit. I was very emotional and as I look back at that experience I was taking the words Coach Bucky was saying to me to personal. I was trying to use it as an excuse to run from the situation instead of accepting the challenge. I went on to finish the summer strong and confident. I would lead my AAU team to the final four of the AAU 14U National Championship in Greensboro, North Carolina. This led to me receiving letters from Division 1 schools all over the country. My first letter came from the University of Clemson. This was a huge confidence booster for me. I was just two years removed from playing organized basketball for the first time. However, I was determined to play college basketball.

I intentionally set clear goals and I read over often. I often stress to individuals, especially kids who play sports, that anything is possible for the individual who's willing to believe in him or herself, who's willing to put in the hard work, and who's willing to be coachable and learn from others that have more experience and wisdom than them. I will later explain in detail my successful key principles that helped me obtain a great level of success throug sports and business. Success is something that an individual must plan for. It's not something that you wish for and it happens. Successfull individuals strategically plan for it, while remaining flexible with how it will be accomplished. As Benjamin Franklin said, *"failing to prepare, is preparing to fail."*

As I entered my first year of private school, I had no clue what I was getting into. I was focusing on playing basketball and getting a scholarship, but I soon realized there was more to it than that. I remember the first day at St. Maria Goretti, my mom had me wear penny loafers to school and boy did I get laughed at all day at school. I came home later that day and told my mom that I couldn't wear these shoes again to school. Kids were laughing at me and making jokes, so she agreed to buying me some timberlands. I was so excited and felt so relieved that I wore them until the rubber came off.

My toughest challenge that I had at St. Maria Goretti was the education side. The teachers demanded excellence from their students. I remember walking down the hallways with my shirt not fully tucked in, and immediately I was called into the office. I need not say any more about that situation...lol! I will just say this: I understood the importance of following the rules and especially the dress code after being pull into the office.

At Goretti, I learned the importance of discipline and striving for excellence not just on the court, but also in the classroom. During my sophomore year of high school, we were about to play

> At Goretti, I learned the importance of discipline and striving for excellence not just on the court, but also in the classroom.

a local public school team that a couple of my friends were playing for.

I was very excited about the opportunity to compete against my childhood friends.

But, it turned out that I was ineligible to play due to my poor grades. You want to talk about a humbling experience! That was one of the toughness and most embarrassing experience that I had to go through as a young kid. I felt bad for myself and my teammates. However, it was just one of those experiences that paid off later in my life. Now that I have kids of my own and as I mentor kids through the game, I can better educate them about the importance of excelling on the court and in the classroom.

As one of my mentors often tells me, failure is just feedback. What it means is that through failure you're given an opportunity to correct your wrongs. See, sitting out that game against my childhood friends gave me the opportunity to correct the wrongs that I made so they did not become a bigger problem later in life.

See, many of us look at failure as a total disappointment, but the reality is it's an opportunity for us to make our adjustments. Those that are successful are willing to fail repeatedly. They aren't expecting to fail, they just understand that it's all a part of the learning curve as they strive for excellence.

As I entered my senior year at St. Maria Goretti, I was told that I would have to go to summer school, which forced me to miss out on playing AAU basketball during one of my most important summers of recruiting. This was a setback, but it eventually it turned into a setup. I would later graduate from Goretti and finish out my high school basketball career as the Tri-State player of the year. As I prepared for the next level I would only take the SAT one time, and my score wasn't high enough to qualify as a Division 1 student athlete, which I was very disappointed about. But little did I know, this too would turn out to be a blessing.

My scores forced me to visit two junior colleges: one in my hometown and the other outside of the city. My mom and I had a meeting set up with the head coach at the local community college. I remember this meeting like it was yesterday. Though I was one of the best players at that time in my area, this coach looked me right in my eyes and said that he didn't think I was good enough to play at that level and only offered me a $200 scholarship.

This is where your belief in yourself comes into play. As you pursue this dream of yours know that there will be naysayers along the path, those that may not think you're capable. However, what you can't do is allow this to distract you from staying the course. I decided to use the coach not thinking that I was good enough as motivation, because deep down, I knew I was more than good enough. I also knew the type of work that I had been putting in to become the player that I was at the time.

So, my next option was to go on a visit to Allegany Community College. One thing that you should know about Allegany is the history of it's men's basketball program. Their history included their winning tradition, National Junior College Tournament appearances, along with their long list of producing high level Division 1 players as well as NBA players.

My high school coach, Cokey Robertson, was a great friend of

Coach Bob Kirk, who was the head coach of Allegany Community College at the time. Coach Robertson was able to set up a tryout for me at Allegany. I did well enough that after the tryout, Allegany offer me a scholarship. It was a great feeling, especially after the disappointing meeting that I had with my hometown junior college.

I had no idea what to expect going into my first year of college basketball. There were six other freshmen who were the go-to players on their high school team that join the team that year. I had to quickly learn how to be a little more unselfish and to do what was best for the team. My first year at Allegany, we were consistently ranked in the top 5 in the national junior college polls. There were a few times where we were ranked #1 overal las well as #1 in defense. We had a unique team that was very talented and determined. I believe if given the opportunity we would have beaten some Division 1 schools.

In our first year, we finished with a record of 30 − 5 and lost in

> My first year at Allegany, we were consistently ranked in the top 5 in the national junior college polls.

the district finals. Our second year, we finished 30 – 3 and made it to the national championship game. At the beginning of our second year, I remember our coach telling those of us who were sophomores to wait until the late signing period to sign with a school, which was April. He had a great feeling that we would make it to the National Junior College Championship Tournament, and fortunate for us, we did. However, we ended up losing in the National Championship game. With us advancing to the national tournament we gain more exposure from D1 schools.

At the time, University of Dayton, University of St. Bonaventure, University of George Mason, and many others were expressing interest in me. Then out of the nowhere, the University of North Texas came into the picture. I remember it like it was yesterday. My coach called me into the office to tell me the University of North Texas was going to offer me a scholarship. He asked what I thought about the opportunity of playing in Texas. I told him to let me think about it. After our conversation I went to the on campus library and began to Google the University of North Texas. I remember pulling up their previous record, and it wasn't good. I believe they had a record of 4-25 and I was thinking to myself I don't know if they would be a good fit for me, especially coming off a two year stretch of winning 60 games and only losing 8 games in two years. I was accustomed to a winning culture. Then I recall going to my teammate Ryan who was from Duncanville, Texas and asked him what he knew about the University of North Texas. He told me that it was a nice campus and that he thought it would be a good fit for me.

I began to ponder the thought of playing for the University of North Texas. I thought about the opportunity of being an intricate part of turning around the program. I had no idea how much work would go into doing that, and I believe I was just a little naïve in that regard. But the next day, I went into the coach's office and told him I had made my decision to play at the University of North Texas. A few days later I would sign my letter of intent to UNT. The intresting thing about all of this is that I signed my letter of intent before I actually took a official visit to see the campus. As you may know you typically go on a visit to the school before you sign a letter of intent. However, I felt in my spirit that it was where I needed to go.

After I signed the letter of intent, the UNT staff set up a visit for me. It all seemed surreal. I had reached my dream of playing Division 1 basketball. They would later fly me out to see the campus. I remember exiting the plane, and feeling the heat wave, I started to wonder what have I gotten myself into. I hadn't ever felt a heat wave like that before. Shortly after the coaches arrived to pick me up to take me to the hotel, which was off campus. I remember walking into my room and walking towards the window where you could see the campus. As I was walking towards the room, I recall the coach asking me if everything was good. I said yes and he proceeded to walk out of the room. As I approached the window that oversaw the campus, I felt as though I had been there before. It was a feeling that I would often get as young kid growing up. I had no idea what it was, but I just remember playing sports or just being in certain situations as if I had already experienced what I was currently experiencing. At that time, I hadn't given my life to Christ. As I look back at that moment, I know it was God giving me confirmation that I had made the right choice.

My first year at UNT was an adjustment for me. I was the only player on the roster that was from out of state, whereas most of my teammates at that time were within driving distance from their home. It was just something that I had to get use to. Another adjustment that I had to make was the way we traveled. In junior college, we rarely traveled long distances except when we were going to tournaments. However, playing Division 1 basketball was the complete opposite. I recall us having to play back-to-back road games my first year. There were times we go several days not attending class due to our schedule. It was tough. I quickly learned to succeed at that level, you have to be both mentally and physically prepared for it.

Our first year, we ended up with a .500 record. We finished up that year with one of the best turnarounds in the NCAA. I recall struggling with being far from home and adjusting to the Texas culture. There were times I wanted to transfer to another school that was a lot closer to home, but my mom would constantly tell me to stick it out. Little did I know at that time, towards the end of my first year is when I would meet my future wife. I

Little did I know at that time, towards the end of my first year is when I would meet my future wife.

remember me and a few teammates deciding to go to IHOP after a school party we attended. As we arrived at IHOP I noticed that the line was very long. So, I took it upon myself to skip past the long line. As I enter IHOP I was looking for an open seat and that's when I notice two young ladies sitting by themselves. So I boldy walked over and sat with them. I was hoping to kill some time until a table became available. The two of them looked at me like "what is this guy doing?"

I began to start a conversation with the two young ladies and I struck a cord with one of them. Eventually, a table would become available for me and my teammates. And after we finished eating, I noticed the two young ladies that I initially sat with walking out at the same time as we were. I proceeded to ask one for them for their phone number. She (Nichole) hesitated at first as if she didn't want to give me her number, but eventually she did and thank God, she did. And a few years later Nichole and I would get married.

My final year at UNT was a struggle but I would finish strong and go on to receive my bachelor's degree. After graduating, I decided to go back home. Since Nichole and I weren't married yet, I just felt it was the right thing to do. Soon after I went out to Detroit, Michigan to try out for a CBA team, unfortunately that opportunity, did not work out. However, later in that year I was as able to join a semipro team in Las Vegas. But little did I know, God would have a different plan. It was 2004 and I had just come back from playing in Las Vegas. I was still holding on the hopes of landing a professional basketball contract overseas.

Often, I would go to the local park to work on my basketball skills. On this day, I decided to make a trip to the park to get some shots up. I remember on this day seeing a young kid shooting on his own on the opposite court from me. I was so focused on getting a good workout in as usual, but I felt something telling me to go over to the other court and give a few pointers to this kid. As I watched him from a distance, I saw him struggling to make shots. So, I decided to go over to him and show him a couple of things that would improve his ability to make more shots. As I left to go back to my court I turned around and notice that he was about take his first shot after I had given him a few tips. As he prepared his hands cor-

> I was so focused on getting a good workout in as usual, but I felt something telling me to go over to the other court and give a few pointers to the kid.

rectly on the ball he took his first shot and swished it. He was all smiles. I just stood in amazement. Later that day, things just felt weird, but I couldn't point it out. That evening I decided to walk down to my cousin's house. Later, me, my cousin and his brother decided to go out to a night club. I wasn't the type that really like going to the clubs as most could tell, I was a homebody, and if I was not playing basketball, I was in the house. As we were driving to the club, things didn't feel right. As we approached the club, tears just began coming down. I didn't know why I was crying. But little did I know, it was the Holy Spirit speaking to me. However, at this time of my life, God was not a priority; it was all about my basketball career for me. My cousin looked back at me as if what is wrong with him. I told them I can't go into the club. They both said "okay cool, we'll go in." And no less than ten minutes later they both came back to the car and I asked them what happened. They said there was nobody in the club. That's when I knew something was going on. It was about 11pm and usually around this time the club would be filled with people.

So, we decided to drive back to the house and as we got there, I said to one of my cousins that I needed him to call Mrs. Loretta.

Mrs. Loretta was someone that I knew had given her life to the Lord and who was very mature in her walk with God. I knew at that moment that I needed to speak with her to see if she could give me more clarity. It was about 11:30pm when I asked my cousin to give her a call. He looked at me and said she's a nurse at the hospital, and they usually have their phones off. I said to him with conviction that she's going answer her phone. He called her two times, and after the second call she called back.

As soon as I got on the phone, I began to share with her what I had experienced earlier that day and up until the call, including the experience that I had at the park with the young kid on the basketball court. After she heard what I had to share, she began to tell me that God was giving me revelation. At that time, I had no idea what she meant. She then said to me that I needed to come to church. I followed her instructions and went to her church that Sunday, which was the next day, and that's when I gave my life to Christ. That's when my life would change and I would begin to see the hand of the Lord move in my life like never before.

During the week, I would go over to the church to pray and to be around the church leaders. The church leaders began to pour

their wisdom into me. I remember feeling condemned and think-

ing that the Lord wouldn't forgive me for my mistakes. I knew

I had made many bad choices in my life up to that point, but I

remember one of the church leaders taking time to share with me

this scripture. Romans 8:1

Therefore, there is now no condemna-tion for those who are in Christ Jesus.

"Therefore there is now no condemnation for those who are in Christ Jesus". When I

heard that, it gave me a sense

of peace and confidence that God still loved me, even with my

shortcomings.

To continue to feed my spirit I purchased a daily devotional,

which is how I learned to understand bible scripture. I would

watch a lot of TD Jakes sermons. I remember just having such

a hunger and thirst for the word of God. As my life began to

change, I decided to that it was the right time to surprise Nichole

and propose to her on Valentine's Day of 2004. So, I flew down

to Texas and booked a car service to pick me up from the airport

to take me to her house. On our way over to her apartment I gave

her a call. I told her that I had sent some flowers to her and they should be dropping them off shortly. Little did she know that I would be in the back seat of the car with the flowers. I called her back and told her the car service was in front of her apartment with the flowers and she needed to go out and get them. After we hung I told the driver to open my door as she got close to the car. As she approached the got close the driver open my door and Nichole scream so loud in shock as she did not expect to see me. I thought for a fact that she was going to wake up the entire neighborhood given it was about close to 10:00pm and a school night.

So, the next day it was Valentine's Day, and I had a plan for how I was going to propose to her. Later that day I told her that I needed to go to Wal-Mart, which was about 10 minutes from her apartment. We went to the mall first to walk around and then we made our way over to Wal-Mart. That's when I told her that I had lost my wallet and that I had to go back to the mall to see if I could find it. But little did she know that I was at her apartment setting up my proposal. I laid rose petals on the floor, and I had bought a rose and

> But little did she know that I was at her apartment setting up my proposal.

put the ring inside the rose. Then I put the rose inside the teddy bear's arm. After I had set up everything, I called her to let her know that I had found my wallet. The truth is I had my wallet with me the entire time.

So, I drove to Wal-Mart to bring her back to her apartment. As we entered her apartment, I let her walk in first. As we got settled inside the apartment, I told her that there was something in her room. That's when she began to follow the rose petals to her room and as she was walking to the room I made sure to be right behind her. She immediately spotted the rose and the teddy bear on her bed. I don't think she was too surprised when she saw the rose and teddy bear. But when she turned around to thank me, I was down on one knee ready, and it was then that I asked her to marry me. She paused for a moment in tears and screamed yes and flung the rose. However, she had know I that the ring was on top of the rose. Thankfully, it didn't take us too long afterwards to find the ring. Without a doubt, this was one of the best days of my life and one of the best decisions I have made. Seeing her face filled with joy and tears brought joy to my heart, as I knew she was the one for me.

Begin with Your Why

There are two great days in a person's life - the day we are born and the day we discover why.

~William Barclay

To some degree we all have the desire to be successful, whether it's with our career, in a sport or it could be just being a better husband, father, wife or mother. We all have the desire of success in us. However, it's up to us to learn how to manifest those desires in our lives. The truth and reality is that some may never experience the success they desire, whether it's due to having a lack of resources or the fear of failing.

People often ask how was I able to build the Lee Green Basketball organization to where it is today. For me it's a simple answer. First it's because of the grace and favor of God. Secondly, I desired it so bad that I would meditate on it daily and I would take the time to plan for it.

As I have heard many successful people quote this *"Success is not a happenstance, it's a plan event".* However, for some who are still stuck it's hard for them to picture themselves being successful.

As you may know achieving success can be challenging but it shouldn't stop us from lacing up our bootstraps so to speak and taking action. Believe in your dream and plan for it. There will be times you will be afraid but you must be willing to do it afraid. Many people

> There will be times you will be afraid but you must be willing to do it afraid

fear because it's unfamiliar territory; they don't know what's on the other side. However, planning can help dissolve some of the fear of the unknown. But as the bible says in 2 Corinthians Chapter five and verse seven, *"For we walk by faith and not by sight..."* Don't allow your circumstances to stop you from taking the initial step. Here's what success looks like. Think of a toddler trying to walk for the first time. What do they typically experience? They experience a lot of falling at the beginning. As I recall my son Jeremiah taking his first steps. I remember how he kept falling and falling but what I don't recall is him crying when he did fall, it was as if he knew to expect to fall. Success is the same way. As you begin to take the initial steps expect to fall because you're walking into uncharted waters. We must do as babies do as they are learning how to walk. They become stronger and more tenacious after each fall. And before you know it they are taking five to six steps in a row. It's the same process as we plan for success we fall and it's our responsibility to learn from each mistake along the way. I'm going to say it again don't let fear stop you from experiencing the success that has been ordained for you.

True success begins when you have discovered your why! Discovering your why can help you overcome many challenges and obstacles that may show up in your life. Have you ever seen someone quit something prematurely, maybe it was because of the pain of failure or maybe they wanted it to happen much faster than it was? Well, when you have a personal WHY you don't just give up so easily especially when you are faced with challenges and setbacks. What you do instead is lean on your why for motivation to overcome the mountain that may be in the way at that moment.

Your WHY gives you the extra energy to push through the pain. You begin to realize it's not about you but it's about the people you may encounter along the path, that will be inspired by your commitment to overcoming the challenges that were presented in your pursuit of discovering your WHY.

We must understand everyone's WHY will not be the same, so don't fall into the trap of comparing your WHY to someone else's. I personally believe that we all have been put on this earth for different purposes. For some it may be coming up with the latest technology or cure for a disease.

For me it was simple my WHY at the early stages of my life was to be the best athlete that I could be. In sports I found peace, joy and excitement. Growing up in a single parent household where my mom would work 12-hour night and day shifts. I would often find myself at home with my sister as my mom was working over night. At those moments I was responbible for helping my mother raise my younger sister. That's when learned what it meant to sacrifice. At that moment I recognized the sacrifice that my mother was making to provide for me and my siblings.

My mother was doing whatever she could to position us for success. Seeing the smile on my mother's face as I scored touchdowns or hearing her scream with excitement when I hit a home-run or do good in basketball. It was those moments that let me know that my WHY had to be bigger than me.

If you have the desire to achieve a great level of success, to the point where you're impacting others in a positive way. Your WHY shouldn't be self-driven; it should be God-driven. If it's self-driven, then ever decision that you make will evolve around you and you only. You have been put on this earth to have a significant impact in

> **Your WHY shouldn't be self-driven; it should be God-driven.**

many people lives not only those that are close to you but others that may be continents away from you. However, it must begin with you developing a clear picture of what your purpose is and once you can define you're PURPOSE it will be much easier to realize it.

So, over these next few chapters my intention is to help you not only discover your WHY but to hopefully inspire you to take the necessary steps to begin living out what God has for you.

How to Discover Your WHY?

"He who has a why to live for can bear almost any how."

~ Friedrich Nietzsche

One of the ways that you can begin to discover your WHY is to look for a problem in the world that you desire to change. Do you know that you're the answer to someone's problem? But you have to first see yourself as the answer or no one else will.

For me as I begin to mature it was right around the time of me graduating college. Soon after I graduated college I begin the quest of playing pro basketball. Around this time an opportunity open up for me to join a semi-pro team in Las Vegas along with a college teammate. I remember it like it was yesterday.

The living conditions were crazy one minute we were staying at the coach's house sleeping on the floor and the next minute we were staying in a hotel. It was then that I knew that playing professionally wasn't for me. I begin to ask myself what do I really want out of this life. In the quest of discovering your purpose there will be moments where you will have to ask yourself what is it that you really want out of this situation or circumstance.

For me it started with the desire of playing pro basketball, which I believed at that time was going to be my purpose in life. I also believed that it would be the vehicle that I could use to give back to my mother and local community. As you begin to get real with yourself by asking this question of "what do I really want out of this life" you will be amazed as things will begin to become much clearer for you.

Discovering your why is an ongoing pursuit. Why, because we are evolving as time passes. As I write this book at the age of 35, my personal mission statment is simple *"Empowering Youth through Leadership, Excellence and Discipline"*. By having a clear picture of my WHY it has allowed me to create a youth basketball organization that not only improves young and adult athlete's basketball skills but most importantly it empowers them for success beyond the game of basketball. Maybe your saying to yourself well I want to do this and this.

The first thing I would suggest for you to do if you're feeling like you have many desires that you would like to accomplish is begin with focusing your energy on one thing and let that one thing evolve with time.

My challenge to you before we move to the next part of this book is to write down 3 things that inspire you and three problems that you see in this world today that you would like to solve.

We are all part of the puzzle all we have to do is discover that one piece and do the best with that piece and let the rest take care of itself. We are not responsible for the how. We are only responsible for believing and acting from that belief.

Planning for Success: Write the Vision

"It doesn't matter where you are coming from. All that matters

is where you are going.

~Brian Tracy

Now that you have discovered your WHY for your life, now you must begin to write the vision. When I first started the Lee Green Basketball program I began writing out my intentions and vision for the program. The bible says in Habakkuk 2:2 "...write the vision and make it plain." As you begin to write the vision no that everything will not be revealed to you right at that moment.

As you start the process of writing the vision down, through the test and trials you will develop a greater clarity for what you desire. Whenever we are pursuing something that is bigger than us uncertainty can creep in and when people feel the sense of un-

...starting the process of writing the vision down you'll begin to gain more clarity and with this clarity will bring certainty.

certainty they often begin to think the worst and they get lost in the how instead of staying focus on the overall vision.

As I have stated before it's not our responsibility to figure out the how. If we were to already know beforehand how things were going to turnout, then we would miss the opportunity to grow and expand our faith. It's in the growing process where you build character, resolve, believe and trust.

Now, how do we begin writing out the vision? In writing the vision this is where you describe how you desire it to look when it has been achieved. Initially, my vision began with me desiring to use the business as an opportunity to spend more time with my wife and kids. As people close to me know family is important to me as so it is to many others, after watching my mom sacrifice working long days and nights and occasionally miss opportunities where you spendg time with me and my siblings. I knew once I began to have kids that my number one priority would be to be fully present in my kid's lives as much as I could. I knew if done right that I could leverage the business to spending quality time with my family. the game of basketball.

I envisioned Lee Green Basketball helping kids succeed on and off the court, in the classroom and outside of the classroom. Also, included in my vision I wanted to go back to the community where I was borned and raised in Hagerstown, Maryland to give other kids the opportunity to realize their dreams. I wanted to be a great example to the kids and show them if I could do it then they could make it as well. Finally, I wanted to give my mom opportunity to help with the basketball organization.

And thus, far I have been fortunate to give to the community that once gave to me. And my mom has played a major role in helping me get things established in my hometown along with my cousin Avery Carey and many other coaches. And due to the growth it has given me the ability to bring my younger sister on board to help with the basketball program in Hagerstown.

The truth is what I just shared with you was not written in the vision. However, this is what I mean when I say all you have to do is just get started. Write the vision out and allow it to evolve with time. It's like

The only limits that exist are the limits that you acknowledge.

planting a flower, all you do is consistently water the

flower and allow the water to do its job and watch the plant grow. It's the same thing with writing your vision. Begin by writing it down on paper and be as specific as you can be. There are no limits. The only limits that exist are the limits that your acknowledging.

As your writing your vision, start visualizing the outcome of your vision. Personally, there would be times where I would visualize my vision at least once a day, by doing so it begin align mind to the endlessly possibilities. See there is no limit to what you can visualize in your mind. Begin using the power of your mind to help you write out your vision. It doesn't have to be a five-page letter. The length of the vision doesn't matter what matters is that you're aligned with it.

My challenge to you is to take 5 minutes of your day to visualize your vision. Then daily begin writing and adding to your vision. Remember this will be an ongoing process. As your vision may change over time as you evolve and have new desires.

Get in the Game

"The future depends on what you do today."

~ Mahatma Gandhi

Now that the vision has been written, now we must begin acting on the vision. A vision without action is like a car sitting in park it's not going anywhere. See it's not enough to get in the vehicle and enter your destination in the navigation while sitting in park. You now must move the vehicle from park to the drive position. This is where you begin to take action. You're probably asking what action should I take, it could be as simple as you

...it's not enough to get in the vehicle and enter your destination in the navigation while sitting in park.

making a phone call. I began calling around to local gyms to reserve practices. Then I begin setting a date for my upcoming tryouts.

As you set the date for when you would like to achieve the desire result. It should encourage you to take action. For some it discourages them because they see it as failure if they don't achieve it on that exact date.

The reality is that you would end up a lot further a long then when you initially started. See the vision will not be realized until you set a date. There is no difference when it comes to realizing your vision; you have to set a date on when you want it to be birthed. For me it was the fall of 2005 when I decided to leave my full-time job. Before then I had the intention of leaving my job but I did not set a date to when I was going to leave. It wasn't until I put a date on it and begin to take the steps to leaving my job and pursing my dream. If I would've never taking action the vision would still be sitting in park.

There's going to be some risk that you will have to take and there are going to be some things that you'll have to sacrifice to realize this vision. For me the sacrifice was getting outside of my comfort of working a 9-5 job that provided me a steady pay check where I knew if I worked "X" amount hours I was going to get paid "X" amount. But when you begin to exercise your faith and take action on something that isn't guaranteed because you have never experienced it before it can bring uncertainty.

This is what you call FAITH IN ACTION. There are many people talking about doing this and that but very few of who taking the action that's needed to birth their vision. The truth is your action is the key to igniting your vision. It's like you're the match and your vision is the gasoline. Your responsibility is to take the step. It's not your responsibility to see the

Your action is the key to igniting your vision.

whole stair case. If that were the case then you would not have the amazing stories of Steve Jobs, Michael Jordan, Oprah Winfrey, Jim Carrey and countless of others who beat the odds and believed enough to take the first step.

Staying in Faith

"There are defining moments in one's life when you learn about yourself, and you deposit that knowledge in the experience account, so you can draw on it at some later date."

~ Jeffrey Archer

In this pursuit of realizing your vision there will be many defining moments that you will encounter. What do I mean by defining moment? A defining moment is when you're at a crossroad or let's say a dead end. You have seen the signs that read "No Outlet", right? Which this means if you were turn down this road there will be no other exit. For me one of my first defining moments is when I had initially taken the leap of Faith of leaving my job. This was just a few months after my wife and I got married and bought our first home. Most people would've never taken the leap because they would've said it's too much risk. As I said earlier if you truly want to impact lives on a level that's bigger then you, while realizing your vision then you will have to take some calculated risk and sacrifice.

For me the risk was worth it. I strongly felt in my heart that the time was now. As I began that journey of building the basketball

> ...you will always have the option of turning back around and doing what's comfortable or stretching outside of yourself and creating another path way.

program a few months later we found out that my wife was a few months pregnant with our son Jeremiah. I began to really feel the pressure. In my mind, I had no choice but to succeed now.

I was faced with a defining moment. Do I give up on the business and begin looking for a 9 to 5 job immediately? or Do I use this as motivation to do what I truly feel in my spirit to do , and build a business that gives me freedom, flexibility and ultimately fulfill my God given purpose. This is what I call a defining moment. You must understand that you will always have the option of turning back around and doing what's comfortable or stretching outside of yourself and creating another path way and not letting the moment define you but you define it.

I encourage you to stay in faith no matter what others say it's like being at a basketball game and the fans are constantly yelling at the referee about a bad call or a non-call. The truth is those referees are so immersed in the game and the moment that they don't have time to listen to what the fans are saying. That's the type of focus you must have when you're realizing your vision. Do not let the ones who are in the stands get you off course. Believe you me you will have always naysayers, doubters, dream killers trying to deter you from living out your dream. Often, they can be your best friends and/or family members. These are the people that want the best for you so to speak but at the same time they don't want to see you get hurt or be disappointed. But you have to be able to overcome that and do what's in your heart to do. So, stay in faith and pursue your vision with determination and focus.

My challenge to you is to write at least one defining moment where you were faced with the option of turning back around and staying in your comfort zone or pushing through.

Take about 5-10 minutes and begin to write that down and how it has changed your life. Then you use those defining moments as a reminder as you continue to press forward to manifesting your dream.

Surround Yourself with Successful People

Don't surround yourself with people who just affirm you. Surround yourself with people who challenge you.

~Tony Robbins

Surround yourself with people who have achieved what you have set out to achieve. They might not have achieved exactly what you would like to achieve but the most important thing is that they have been through the process of overcome challenges and still succeeding. These type individuals have develop successful habits and the knowledge that they have gained over time can be of great help to you. The reality is if you're the smartest person in your circle then you will always feel as though you're on an island by yourself.

The importance of surrounding yourself with successful individuals is that it can and will shorten up the learning curve, it will also help you avoid the similar **... you must become** pit falls that they may have ex- **a great listener.** perienced. There's no need to try and reinvent the wheel when you don't have to. As you begin seeking out these individuals you must become a great listener. I recall many of times where I would reach out to my mentors to receive guidance in regards to my business. I would ask them questions to get their perspective and wisdom. As I began to listen to their feedback I quickly learned the importance of becoming a great listener. I began to develop a habit of taking notes as I engaged in dialog with them. What you'll learn about those individuals who are very successful in their field is that they are great listeners which makes them effective communicators.

Once I began to put myself around successful and intelligent individuals such as Bishop E. Bernard Jordan and many others who have poured their wisdom and experiences in me, I immediately noticed my business and spiritual walk begin to accelerate. You must understand the vision that you have will not be accomplished alone. You have to set in your mind that though you may hold the vision it will take you sharing the vision with others, so they can assist you in carrying out the vision. Where most people fall short is when they try doing it alone and I fell into the same trap but quickly learned that I will never be successful with that mind set. Pride can be an individual's down fall. Refuse to allow pride to stop you from seeking the advice of others who have gone before you. If you were to read up on any successful person in any particular field one thing that I can guarantee you is this they all had at least one individual that they would say played a vital role in their success.

A while back a saw a video on YouTube and it was video of Michael Jordan and he was hosting a basketball camp and one of the campers asked him if he had one game to play who would he want to coach him Phil Jackson or Dean Smith. And like many I would have immediately have said Phil Jackson because of the all the championship rings he won with Phil Jackson being his coach, but instead Michael said Dean Smith and he begin to elaborate on why he would choose Dean Smith. As I paraphrase he said that Dean Smith was the reason why he was able to become the player that he became in the NBA because of his coaching and mentorship.

We all need a coach or coaches in our life. In like I mention, before the coaches, mentors and teachers come into your life to assist in you realizing your dream. These individuals aren't always highly successful people, but the one ingredient that you want them to have is some level of experience of success and failure. See an individual can only share to the degree of what they have experience.

Always surround yourself with individuals who will challenge you and elevate you to become better then you are today. And get rid of those toxin individuals that are always speaking negative, complaining and pulling you down whether it be directly or indirectly. You have probably heard this saying before, *"you are the some totally of the 5 closes people you hang with the most"*.

You'll notice if you hang around an individual long enough you'll begin to use the same language that they use. If they are speaking negative then you don't want that negativity to creep into your spirit, which could possibly prevent you from accomplishing your dreams and goals.

My challenge to you is to write down at least 2-3 names of individuals that you can begin to reach out to and share your vision in hopes of gain their wisdom and knowledge. This will begin to expand your horizons and create endless possibilities of you achieving your vision.

Stay Committed to the Process

Be committed to the process without being emotionally attached to the results. (Unknown)

The journey is what shapes and molds us. It teaches us things that we would have never known if we would have never gone through the journey. Many people can get lost in the journey because they are so consumed with the outcome or result. When I say, they are consumed with the outcome let me go a little deeper into this. What I'm referring to is that they have already made up in their mind how it should all unfold. And if doesn't unfold the way they have envision it they then give up prematurely. The reality is we don't know exactly how it will turn out. Our responsibility is to believe and stay committed to the process.

If you ever get the opportunity read the book title "Three Feet from Gold" by Sharon L. Lechter and Greg S. Reid. There's a quote in the book that reads *"If you have a big enough reason to do something, the 'how' will simply show itself."* This quote is a reminder that all we have to do is take action on what we believe and the rest will take care of itself. All I knew about building

> ## Be committed to the process without being emotionally attached to the results.

a business from ground up wasn't very much. It wasn't as if I group around family members who had or built there own businesses.

However, I remained consistent with the belief of this is what I was called to do and with that I continue to take consist action. There will be many obstacles and detours along the way however the one thing that you cannot allow to be shaken is your belief, therefore we must stay committed to the process. The bible reads in Hosea 4:6 *"my people are destroyed for the lack of knowledge."* It's what you don't know that can eventually set you back.

The process reveals to you what you don't know so that you can learn what to do when approached with a similar situation. And what you do know you have to use to your best ability. What I quickly learned throughout this journey of pursuing my dream while creating opportunities for our others, is the importance of staying with the process. We must become great at getting back up. I remember when I had my first official tryout only two kids showed up. However, I had 20 players pre-registered at that time, so I went in expecting 20 players to show up but instead only two showed up. See I could have been so emotionally attached to the outcome and I would've missed out on an opportunity to learn a valuable lesson. Before you can be elevated to the next level you must go through the test. The test comes to reveal how committed you are to your own vision.

When I saw that only two showed up I was disappointed but I quickly moved from disappointment to seizing the moment mode. I realized that this was my opportunity to prove to myself how much I was committed to **...don't let the** realizing my vision. I can now **moment define you** say since that moment of time, **but instead you de-** our program through the grace **fine it.** of God typically has about 100 – 200 kids attending each of our tryouts.

It's amazing how those two kids became 100+ kids. We are presented with the opportunities to plant seeds into our vision. The vision is like the soil and your defining moments are the seeds.

Be committed to your defining moment and watch your vision grow into something would have never imagined.

My challenge to you is when you're faced with a defining moment, be committed to the process and don't let the moment define you but instead you define it.

The Power of Focus

"If you keep doing what you've always done, you'll keep on getting what you've always got."

As it pertains to your focus you must begin to make it a priority to focus your energy on those things that will push you closer to the realization of your vision. Focus begins with you prioritizing the things that are most important first. For me it was building a business that would give me the leverage to spend quality time with my wife and kids, without being strapped to a 9 to 5 job, where in most cases you have no flexibility.

Keep in mind the decisions that you will have to make in regards to your vision should be made with the WHY front and center. You will be presented with opportunities that will look enticing but in the end will not benefit you. Stay focus on the task at hand. There have been many times where I fell for the bait of seeking new opportunities thinking that it would push me closer to my goal. However, those opportunities cause me to get off course and lose focus on the real task at hand.

What helped me to stay on course was when I began writing out specific and attainable goals. By doing this it gave me daily actionable goals that would continue to push me forward. Now, as I was beginning to expand the business one of my goals was to begin hiring new coaches. At the time, I had never hire anyone before but I knew that it was a necessary step to take if I was going to live out my vision.

Their will be times where you will have to take calculated risk that will cause you to get out of your comfort zone and do something that you have never done before. I know if I didn't take on the challenge of hiring new coaches that it could have possibly delayed my success.

In the book The Power of Focus by Jack Canfield it said *"If you make the effort to develop the habit of unusual clarity, the pay- off for you down the road will be tremendous"*. You must have a clear picture of what it is that you truly want if you don't you will feel as though you're moving but not making any progress. I personally have been in this position before and it felt as though I was making the right decisions and moving in the right direction but little did I know I was moving but with very little progress. I remember as I begin bringing on new coaches and soon after things begin going downward. I had the right intention but I had been hiring the wrong coaches. Their motives and intentions did not align with my vision.

With that I had disgruntle coaches, parents and players. What I soon realized is that I could not blame the coaches for this chaos, I had to look at myself and where I went wrong. Maybe I could have been a little clearer on what the expectation was.

The reason why I mention this is that you're not going to get it right at the beginning. You're going to make mistakes the key is to minimize those mistakes. Which is why having a clear focus and picture of the end result will help you make better decisions.

Start today by making it a priority to laser your focus, get a clearer picture of the end result.

Be Flexible

"The measure of a person's strength is not his muscular power or strength, but it is his flexibility and adaptability."

— *Debasish Mridha*

As you develop this crystal clear picture of the end goal, you must remain flexible with how it will show up in your life. As I was on my quest to creating a life that provided me flexibility and purpose. I had clear picture of which vehicle could create that opportunity for me and it was why I started my youth basketball organization. The mission of the youth basketball organization was to provide an opportunity for kids to improve their basketball skills while learning valuable life skills that could assist in their success beyond the game of basketball.

However, if you would have told me that in this process of building the program that I would come close to losing my home to foreclosure, I probably would have never taken the initial step to start the program. As I was going through that experience I was feeling like I had no control of the situation. Have you ever been in a situation where you felt things were spiraling out control so much so that you will never find a way out of the situation? That's exactly how I felt as I was beginning to expand and grow the program. As the man and leader of the house I felt as though I could not show any signs of helplessness. My wife and kids were counting on me to provide for them.

However, I was determine to seeing this vision all way through. I had no idea how it was going to happen but deep down I knew this is what God had called me to do. I remember at the very beginning as we were getting the word out about our program, me and my wife would get up early and go house to house putting flyers in people's mailbox. We would go to local fitness centers and put flyers on people's vehicles. Our desire to succeed and grow the business was so strong that we were willing to do whatever it took at the moment to make it become a reality.

See the truth is there is no better teacher then you going through the actual process itself. You learn so much more about yourself when you are committed to going through the process. If I would have known before I had gotten started in this pursuit of building this business that I would have to go through these different challenges and obstacles, I probably would never have left my job. Which is why I'm thankful that God hid some things from me at the beginning so I could stay focus on the task at hand. Therefore, I believe you should focus only on that which you can control.

But do understand everyone's path will be different. As I going through the different challenges, such as not making enough money to pay my mortgage or put gas in the vehicles. See these are things that people don't see when one is building a business. Which is why I am so amazed of how much our basketball program grown over the years. We now have multiple locations in multiple states. It's all because the grace and favor of God.

The one mistake that I often made was getting too consumed with how it was going to happen. This resulted in me making some poor decisions along the way that could have been prevented early on, not that I regret any of those decisions it was a learning curve that I had to go through. I soon recognized that I was trying too hard to make the dream happen which most do. I was leaning to my own understanding and now 100% trusting the Lord with vision and provision. I found myself often trying to take matters into my own hands.

Whatever, it is that you have the desire to achieve in your life just remember your job is to believe and take appropriate action from that belief and trust that the Lord will take care of the rest. You will not achieve this dream by yourself; it will take the assistance of others. Which is why you must remain flexible and allow God to position you as you take consistent action.

By leaving the how to the Lord it allowed me to learn the essential principles to building a sustainable and profitable business. I know it's easier said than done but believe you me all God wants from us is to see us fully trust him throughout the process.

In Proverbs 3:5-6 it reads *"Lean not to own understanding but trust the Lord with all your heart."* As you begin to surrender the vision to the Lord and allow him to guide you the outcome will always be in your favor.

My 10 Keys to Achieving Success

Setting Goals

"Plan your work for today and every day,

then work your plan."

One of the keys that I contribute to my success to is goal setting. I'm constantly writing and refining my goals. It's important that you set clear and achievable goals. You'll have some audacious goals that you'll want to achieve. However, you must begin with a systematic approach. I recommend chunking the big goals down into bite sizes. What I mean by this is taking the time and breaking your major goals into small actionable steps.

For example, one of my goals was to write this book within 30 days. That was the big goal so I managed to break this goal down into small action steps that would assist me with

By setting small actionable goals it allows us to remain confident while we build momentum.

achieving my goal of writing this book in less than 30 days. The first step was to research how many words it would take to write a 100 to 200-page book. In my research, I discovered that it would take about 40,000 to 50,000 words to write a 100 to 200-page book. From there I made a small actionable goal to write at least 3,000 words a day. I knew if I remained consistent with that goal I would have written over 60,000 words, which is more than enough.

If you master this one concept your goals will no longer seem to far fetch. This concept will encourage you to take more action. We often fail to achieve our goals because they seem too far out of our reach which can lead to dissatisfaction. This leads to inaction and many people giving up on the goal entirely. By setting small actionable goals it allows you to remain confident and at the same time build momentum.

One quick note be sure that your goals are indeed obtainable. What does a pet owner typically do to reinforce a behavior that they want their pet to repeat, they give them a treat? It's like that with any pet when you reward it with a treat it reinforces the desired behavior. It's the same way with us humans the small actionable goals keep us not only excited but it reinforces the desired behavior which helps in accomplishing our goal.

The purpose of our goals is to inspire us to take action and to give us the ability to measure our progress. However, the one mistake that most individuals make is setting goals that are so big that it causes them to become discourage. Your goals are there to inspire and to motivate you, not to discourage you.

As you begin to write out your goals know that it may not show up the way that you initially wrote it down. Remain flexible with your goals and adjust your goals accordingly as you take action. Your goals should always be moving you forward and not backwards. As Benjamin Franklin once said, *"Failing to plan is planning to fail"*.

The bible reads in Habakkuk 2:2 "Write the vision and make it plain." When you take the time to write down your goals down and simplify them into small actionable steps, watch how much easier it will be to achieve them.

Start today by writing out your goals then simplify them into 2 to 3 actionable steps, which should inspire you to take consistent action.

If You Can See it, You Can Achieve it

"Meditation is the tongue of the soul and the

language of the spirit."

Another key that I contribute my success to is meditation. I make it a point for when I wake up to immediately begin meditating and imagining my goals. I visualize myself achieving each goal and I get into the feeling of what it would feel like once the goal has been achieved. I make it a point to meditate on each goal before I go to sleep. By imagining the end result it allows me to go through my day enhancing my ability to recognize opportunities that align with my goals.

Meditation helps me become more confident especially when I'm faced with obstacles along the way. Meditation has helped me focus my attention on the process and not the how. When you take the time to meditate it begins to take your mind off the how and refocus it on the process. As you learn to apply meditation to your life you will quickly learn that you don't necessary have to have all the resources at that present moment to take the steps towards living a life that you so desire.

Whether it's starting a business, leaving a job to pursue a greater dream or maybe you desire to receive a college athletic scholarship. Regardless of what your desire is meditation can assist in you achieving it. The bible reads in Joshua 1:8 *"Study this Book of Instruction continually. Meditate on it day and night so you will be sure to obey everything written in it. Only then will you prosper and succeed in all you do."*

I contribute some of my success as a basketball player to meditation. The night before the game I would sit quietly and play the game through my mind as if I was playing the actual game. During my meditation, I would put myself in situations that I would most likely be in during the actual game. I did this so when it came time to play the actual game I would be best equipped for my instincts to take over.

Joseph Murphy in his book the Miracle Power of Your Mind mentions that *"the road inward is the road to greatness."* The true power relies on the inside not on the outside. See many

...the true power and work is done before you take the physical action

people get too caught up in the work of their hands. However, the true power and work is done before you take the physical action and it can be done through meditation. If we would learn how to use the power of meditation to our advantage it would be much easier to achieve our goals. But the problem is we get to busy with our day to day activities whether it's planning the next strategy for our business or taking our kids to their next sporting event. Which results in us never taking the time to quiet our minds. So much so that we lose sight of being present and appreciating the little things that brings fulfillment to our lives.

We often fail to be present in our conversations. So much so that our minds are often drifting off to what we have to do next instead of being present and enjoying the conversation. Meditation has been a great help in my success and ability to stay focus and present each and every day.

I challenge you to begin by taking 5-10 minutes before you go to sleep and when you first wake up to meditate on you achieving the desires of your heart. Again, you must be consistent in meditating it's as simple spending five minutes a day. Once every three weeks won't be as effective as doing it daily or at least every other day.

Become A Great Follower

"He who cannot be a great follower, cannot be a great leader."

~Aristotle

A nother key to my success has been through the different mentors that have shown up in my life, such as Bishop E. Bernard Jordan, who has helped me in more ways than one. He has helped me improve as leader, a father and business owner. He has challenged me to get outside of my comfort zone and to dream bigger. He continues to challenge me to stretch outside my comfort zone in regards to me growing in my personal relationship with Christ.

When I first met Bishop E. Bernard Jordan I was about three years into establishing my basketball program and I was still going through the infant stages of the business. But after a couple of one on one coaching sessions with my mentor my business began to take off. I begin to insert the wisdom that he would often share with me and my program began to triple in the number of kids that joined my program. In addition I was blessed with the opportunity to expand my program into other states.

Having a mentor is priceless. It can and will shorten the learning curve, which is why I believe that everyone should have a coach. If Michael Jordan had a coach and he was one of the greatest players who ever played in the NBA, if not the greatest player then we should invest in a coach.

As my mentor and business coach explained to me the coach comes to reveal your blind spots. We all have blind spots in are life and often it takes another individual to point them out to us. It's like a coach sitting on the sidelines and a player playing in the

> **The blind spots are the spots that we can't see ourselves because we are often too consumed with the business, the idea, or the goal.**

game. The player has a narrow view of things because he or she sees it only through their eyes. Where as a coach on the sideline has a wider view because he or she must see everything to put individual players and the team in the best position to succeed. The blind spots are the spots that we can't see ourselves because we are often too consumed with the business, the idea, or the goal.

Another mentor who has helped me continue to grow as a business owner and family man is Thomas Whitaker. Thomas is a very successful businessman who understands the importance of family. One of the many things that I have been able to learn from him is not only what it takes to build a successful business but the importance of not forgetting about your family during the journey. I have watched how he consistently incorporates his family with his businesses while still making the time to attend his sons sporting events and as well as spend time with his wife. It's inspiring to see someone close to you who has had a lot of success on many levels and who remains a consistent model of success.

A mentor is essential to your overall success and development. Be on the lookout for those individuals that you can lean on and gain wisdom from. They don't have to be in the same business or field that you're in. Though my business revolves around basketball and kids the reality is my mentors are not in the same field of business that I'm in. However, the wisdom they share with me through their experiences can still be applied to my businesses.

To become a great leader one must become a great follower. Having a mentor teaches one how to follow, listen and take in instruction. If you look at any of the great successful men and women in our world today most of them have had a mentor at some point in their life whom have helped them grow into the individual that they are today. When I think of great mentors and mentees I think of Joshua and Moses, David Robinson and Tim Duncan, Bobby Knight and Coach K and many others.

When you look at Joshua and Moses who were intricate people in the bible, you immediately look at how Moses was a great example for Joshua to carry out the purpose God had for the Israelites. Through the wisdom of Moses and the grace of God Joshua was able to lead the Israelites over the red sea. After Moses die Joshua became the next leader and he went on to become a great leader.

At some point in our lives we will need guidance and direction. I believe as we begin to pursue our purpose that God has for us along the journey he will raise individuals up to help us. Then it becomes our responsibility to recognize who these individuals are so we can maximize the mentorship. With that said, we must become aware of the individuals who enter our lives, so we can be ready to receive guidance and wisdom from them. Great leaders know they can't accomplish this mission by themselves. They know in trying to do so can lead to burnout and frustration.

I learned to become a great listener as I connected with my mentors. Too often we miss out on opportunities because we are too quick to speak and as result we fail to take the time to listen with not only our ears but with our eyes.

Begin to look for individuals that you can learn from as you pursue your dreams and aspirations. Having a great mentor will help you avoid having to go down the wrong path and waste time going through the same mistakes of those that have gone before you.

Fall and Get Back Up

"Winners are not people who never fail but who never quit."

As you pursue this dream of yours, it's important that you develop perseverance. There will be times where you will be faced with a number of challenges and test during your pursuit. These challenges come to help

> You don't know how strong your faith is until your faith has been tested.

you develop your inner strength. You don't know how strong your faith is until your faith has been tested. The test comes to reveal to us what we do and do not know. The test also comes to test our commitment to the dream. Most of us quit at the first sign of a challenge. Then there are others who will do whatever it takes to realize their dream.

There were many times that I would've preferred to not face the obstacles and test that came my way. Whether it was the transitioning from playing football to playing basketball or hiring new coaches. However, through those challenges I have gained a greater appreciation of the process and what it takes to be successful. I learned some valuable lessons that I can now share with others. And I will continue to learn valuable lessons as I strive to go higher in my purpose. As we are faced with new challenges these challenges it will cause us to go deeper from within. As I quote my mentor *"...go within or go without."* Success is an inside job and not an outside job. When we are, battle tested, we can withstand more. Therefore, NFL players go through two-a-days to prepare for their upcoming season. Two-a-days are where they have two practices in a day, one in the morning and one in the late afternoon. Why, so they can be battle tested for the long grueling football season.

With that said, expect challenges to come your way, because without them it would be difficult to develop our inner strength and learn the valuable lessons which will assist us in going to the next level in our purpose. Don't succumb to the challenges and adversity that you may face. Believe me there is a greater purpose.

I have learned that success is to be measured not so much by the position that one has reached in life as by the obstacles which he has had to overcome while trying to succeed. ~ Booker T. Washington

Take Consistent Action Daily

"Action always beats intention."

Consistent action is what separates the achievers from the non-achievers. You will always have the option of either pressing on or quitting. You can believe for the dream, you can meditate on it, you can speak it, but if you fail to take consistent action towards the dream you will not see the dream through. Faith without action is dead. When you mix faith with action is when you will have success.

As you develop the habit of taking consistent action you will begin to notice patterns. In these patterns, you will know what necessary adjustments to make. This doesn't me you won't have setbacks or miss the mark occasionally. Many people today are sitting on the sidelines and failing to enter the game. They say things like "I have to wait until I have the money" or "I have to wait until I meet the right person." While those who believe say the opposite. They say to themselves, "I'm going to move on what I do know at this moment and trust God with the rest."

Consistent right action will lead to success. Why because when you're on the court playing the game you have more opportuni-

Consistent action will eventually lead to success.

ties to learn while being in the game. When you develop the habit of taking consistent action you are building momen-

tum. To achieve a great level of success you must have momentum on your side. Success loves speed. As the great writer, Sun Tzu puts it *"the later you start, the more you require."* No more standing on the sidelines get in the game and begin to act on your dreams and aspirations.

When I was faced with the challenge of building a business from the ground up, I could have used the excuse of not having any business experience, not having enough money and so on. But instead I acted on what I knew at that time. Of course, there were times I wanted to quit, however when you are focus on taking action you don't have time to focus on what you do not have.

Too many of us want people to feel sorry for us. In the bible, Joshua was faced with a challenge. He was taking consistent action towards the purpose that God had called him to. He was consistently winning battles until he came up on a battle that he just knew he was going to win, but this time he ended up losing this battle. He couldn't figure out why God would allow him to lose a battle that he shouldn't have loss. But little did he know it wasn't God that had caused him to lose the battle, it was someone in his camp that broke protocol, who stole something that belong to God. In Joshua chapter 7, God gave Joshua specific instructions to give to his people. And it was to not to take from the land of Jericho after they defeated them. But Achan decided to take from the land which resulted in Joshua losing the next battle against AI.

After the defeat, Joshua fell on his knees asking God why he allowed him to lose, it was then when God revealed to him that someone in his camp took from the land of Jericho. See Joshua was looking for self-pity from God but instead God reacted differently and in Joshua 7:10, God told Joshua "...to get up off his face."

> Discouragement can lead to inaction if you stay discourage to long and inaction will lead to no growth.

Then immediately he told him to find the one who stole from him.

There is no doubt that God feels are pain, but he doesn't want us to be in self-pity, instead he wants us to take consistent action towards the purpose that he has called us towards just like he did Joshua. Discouragement can lead to inaction if you stay discourage to long and inaction will lead to no growth. Be persistent in your action and believe *"...that all things work together for the good of those who love God and who are called according to his purpose"* Romans 8:28.

.

Obedience Is Better Than Sacrifice

"I don't see success as the goal but obedience as the goal."

You're ability to follow instruction will be the exact result of the level of success that you will experience in your lifetime. Quite often there will be times God will instruct you to do something that will be unconventional to the natural eye but to the one

> You are ability to follow instruction will be the exact result of the level of success that you will experience in your lifetime.

who is in tuned with the spirit of God, it will make total sense. I recall a time when God challenged me to give a significant financial seed into a church, the amount was way above what I was use to giving. Though I was a little nervous to follow through I went ahead and did it anyway. I understood the importance of obedience, but I also knew that I had the desire to build a business that was bigger than me. I believed by obeying and planting this significant financial seed that it would possibly open up opportunities for my business to expand in more ways that I could have ever imagined.

In the bible, it reads *"Give, and you will receive. Your gift will return to you in full pressed down, shaken together to make room for more, running over, and poured you're your lap. The amount you give will determine the amount you get back"* Luke 6:38 (NLT).

Whenever you desire to achieve something that is greater than you it's will cause you to stretch your faith. There hasn't been a time when I made a commitment to go to another level whether it was in my marriage, finances, business, friendships, that I wasn't challenged to do something that was outside of my comfort.

When I think of obedience I think of Abraham's servant who Abraham gave the instruction to go and find his son Isaac a wife in Genesis Chapter 24:4 (NLT) the servant said *"But what if I can't find a young woman who is willing to travel so far from home..."*. The servant had doubts that he could find Abraham's son a wife but the servant went ahead and obey the instruction any way and in the end, he found Isaac a wife.

1 Samuel 15:22 "...to obey is better than sacrifice."

Don't Be Afraid of Change

"Life is a series of natural and spontaneous changes. Don't resist them; that only creates sorrow. Let reality be reality. Let things flow naturally forward in whatever way they like."

~Lao Tzu

Another important key to achieving a great level of success is adaptability. One must learn how to adapt to different situations that may occur along the journey. For example, when I made the decision to play Division 1 basketball at the University of North Texas I knew that I was going to state that was unfamiliar to me at the time. Up until that point I had never been to the state of Texas. The furthest that I had been south was North Carolina. I understood that this would put me far away from family and relatives. Coming from the east coast to the south was a major adjustment. I had to adjust to the pace which was much slower and I wasn't prepare for the hospitality and the kindness of the people. I was use to putting my head down and minding my own business. It was a complete culture shock for me. However, through this experience it taught me the importance of being flexible and adapting to new surroundings. It was challenging at the beginning both socially and mentally in regards to basketball. As it relates to basketball I was coming off an experience in Junior College, where we won 90% of our games in

...we won 90% of our games in the two years that I was there. In our final year, we made it to the National JUCO Cahmpionship game and loss by three points.

the two years that I was there. In our final year, we made it to the national championship game and loss by three points. Prior to me attending UNT there men's program had had several losing seasons. In their previous season upon me arriving they had a win loss record of 4-29.

With that said, I was force to adapt to a different environment then what I was accustom to. It's not to say that one must 100% accept it but instead be willing to learn from the experience so that one could be better prepared for the next experience. I believe there are stages or levels to success that we all must go through if we truly desire to be considered high achievers. Most people try to avoid the process because they aren't willing to adapt. There are times that we should put ourselves in uncomfortable situations to bring the best out of us. By doing so can cause us to expand our thinking. This can lead us to creating new ideas and possibilities. Choosing to go into an unfamiliar part of the country did an exactly that for me, it forced me to expanded my thinking for what I thought was possible. What I quickly discovered about myself is that I could adapt to being in an unfamiliar situation while being far away from family and still succeed. I soon realized that anything is possible to the one who is willing to be believe and not be afraid of change.

What comes to my mind when I think of person who resembles adaptability is a coach specifically one who coaches a team sport? As you may know being a coach can be a tough and challenging job. Coaches are evaluated based on their wins and loss record. When you win most believe you're a good coach but when you lose most think you're not a good coach. It's all based on perspective. However, as a coach the challenge is being able to adapt to the ups and downs throughout the game. Things can be going very well for the coach and their team the first quarter and then in the second quarter things can quickly change. Whenever you watch a coach, who has the ability to adapt to the different circumstances that are being presented to them throughout the game, what stands out is their ability to make in game adjustments at the right time. They don't get caught up in the emotions of the game as they know they must stay locked in and be ready to make in-game adjustments.

It works the same way for you and I. As you embark on this journey of success in pursuit of your God given purpose you must remain calm as life will bring you challenges, highs and lows. Do avoid making important decisions when your emotions are high, this is where we make poor decisions.

Think of opportunities where you can place yourself strategically that can assist in you learning how to adapt, be flexible and think outside of the box of the endless possibilities.

Master the Art of Self-Discipline

For the moment all discipline seems painful rather than pleasant, but later it yields the peaceful fruit of righteousness to those who have been trained by it.

Hebrews 12:11 ESV

Suffer the pain of discipline or suffer the pain of regret. We are faced with decisions in life daily such as choosing to continue to put off what we know to do or disciplining ourselves and doing what we should do. Many of us want the reward but avoid going through the process of what it will take to obtain the reward. The success that one experiences in their lifetime can be traced back to their self-discipline.

We watch athletes on television like Michael Jordan, Kobe Bryant, Tom Brady and countless others and we are amazed by their achievements. But what we fail to acknowledge is their self-discipline. We don't see the countless hours of hard work that they are putting in every morning, whether it's lifting weights, eating proper foods, shooting hundreds of jump shots before or after practice or researching and preparing for interviews like Oprah Winfrey continues to do so she can deliver the best interview while keeping her audience engaged.

We all dream of being successful but very few take the time to discipline ourselves to get to where we ultimately want to be in life. I recall having the desire to play Division 1 college basketball at the age of 13. I was committed to the dream so much so that I became obsessed with it. That's when I begin to study the great players and their habits that got them to level that I was-dreaming of playing one day.

Suffer the pain of discipline or suffer the pain of regret.

I would sacrifice hanging out with friends just so I could work on my jump shot and improve my ball handling skills. What I begin to realize is that there were other young inspired athletes who had a similar vision. I instantly knew that I wasn't just competing from within but I was competing against players from all over the world who had a similar dream. So, I begin to discipline myself more than ever and I would create my own work plans. However, in today's day and age our kids have more opportunities to receive individual training from experienced athletes such as myself. However, when I was coming up I didn't have that opportunity. I had to discipline myself to get up and train on my own. Whether, it was running hills at the local park or shooting jumpers with the weighted vest. Looking back at those moments of my life and when I received my first college basketball letter from the University of Clemson I knew that it was due to the hard work that I had been putting in.

Success doesn't wait for anyone. You must not only discipline yourself for it but you must mustard up the strength to seize it. I remember reading a quote by John Maxwell that reads *"Small disciplines repeated with consistency every day lead to great achievements gained slowly over time."* The truth is at that time I had no idea when my opportunity was going to show up. However, I consistently did the small things that would later yield me the opportunity to play Division 1 basketball.

Too many of us get so consumed with the end goal that we fail to realize that it's the small achievements that will lead us to our greatest achievements. And for most of us when we don't immediately see the return on our hard work we quit and move on to something that were not as passionate about which then leads to disappointment.

As I began building my business I started with a simple goal of replacing my income. And I figured out what I needed to do in order to accomplish it.

After you have master self-discipline you then need to develop a great level of patience with the process. In the bible, there's a verse in Ecclesiastes chapter three verse 2 where it reads "...*a time to plant and a time to harvest.*" What I gain from this scripture is there will be a time to plant which is the hard work and self-discipline. Then there will be a time to harvest and that's when you will take action. But we first must plant the seed of hard work. And we must live in great expectation while we continue to put in the small disciplines daily. Where you find consistency, you will also find discipline. Where there is no consistency there is no discipline.

I challenge you to find that one thing that you will be committed to doing over these next several days and focus your energy on that until it becomes a habit. As you set small obtainable goals you will give yourself the opportunity to develop good consistent habits. However, do not fall into the trap of trying to do a million things at once. In doing so, you will discover chaos and frustration. Discipline is your friend it's not some-

were.

I recall another time where I took the leap of faith to purchase our 2009 Mercedes Benz at that moment never in my life had I ever owned a luxury car such as a Mercedes. I remember dreaming as a little kid of one day possibly owning a luxury car but even then, it felt so farfetched. At this moment of time it was a stretch of our faith because at the time we did not have the resources to purchase the Mercedes however I knew that if God had done it before that he would do it again. I was just moving by faith as the Lord instructed me to do so.

So, I woke up one morning and I begin to search for some car dealerships to call. I was specifically looking for a black on black Mercedes which was my wife's dream car. As I begin to call around to the dealerships there was one specific dealership that I connected with and before I went to this dealership I called another dealership and asked them if they had a black on black Mercedes and they said no not at this moment.

So, I decided to go to the dealership that had the black on black Mercedes on their lot so I could test drive it. Once I arrived to the dealership they took me to the back to show me the vehicle.

I requested to take it for a test drive after I came back from the test drive, I told them that I would like to move forward with the purchase the vehicle. It took about an hour for them to get all the paperwork submitted but unfortunately, they were unable to approve me for the loan. Though I was a little disappointed I chose to remain confident. I got back into my car and headed home.

As I begin to drive a few miles down the road my phone rings and it just so happen to be the second dealership who had originally said they did not have a black on black Mercedes on their lot. As I answered the phone they said that they were calling to let me know that they just had a used 2009 black on black Mercedes pull up on their lot. That's when I immediately asked them when could we come by to test drive it. They gave me the okay to come by that same day.

After I hung up with them I call my wife and told her that I was coming home to pick her up, so we could go and test drive the Mercedes. So, my wife and I went to the dealership and as we got closer to the dealership she was too afraid to test drive the car. In her mind, she did not want to do any damage to it. So, I took it for a test drive with the sales person in passenger seat and my wife in the back. After taking the vehicle around the block a few times I drove it back to the dealership. Instantly, we knew that this was the one for us. They submitted the paperwork and a few hours later we were approved for the loan and that day we drove off the lot with my wife's dream car.

I share these stories with you because my wife and I are no different than anyone else; if God can do it for us then he can do it for you. It's our belief that determines what we receive in our life time. If we can learn to master our thoughts and have faith, we can change the circumstances in our life. This is not to say that things aren't going to be challenging along the way but we can change the way we view those challenges that come into our life by seeing them in a way that we know we can overcome them.

We must be careful with not allowing others to project their negative and self-limiting beliefs on us. If you allow it people will press their limiting beliefs on you whether it's indirectly or directly. Which is why it's important that you pay close attention to who you allow to have your ear. Some people are okay with settling with a life of mediocrity and they get upset and intimidated when they see people like you and I who are stretching themselves and believing for the impossible and achieving them.

Deep down those same people who speak against your success are the same ones who really want to experience what you are experiencing but instead they allow their self-doubts override their faith.

My thought is this what's the worst thing that could happen that I get told no we can't approve you for this loan or you're not qualified. We all have been told the word no before but for some odd reason we tend to take the no more personal the older we become. However, when we were kids we would often hear the word no hundreds of times but it never stopped us from continuing to pursue what we truly wanted.

I experience this exact thing with my kids quite often, especially my two older kids. They will keep coming back to me and wife until they get a yes and honestly though it may bother me at times, however, I love their persistence and their commitment to receiving the yes. As my wife and I know as they get older they will hear the word no more often than they have heard it from us.

again and it does not have to be with the same person or company but I do want you to pursue the yes. You will be amazed of how quickly you will receive the yes.

What Is FEAR?

"Don't let the fear of what could happen

make nothing happen."

What is fear? I recall reading an interview where Kyrie Irving was giving his description of what fear was to him. He said, "Fear is just a product of your imagination." I believe this to be true. What we fear can be traced back to our imagination. Often it can be instilled in us during our adolescences from our parents, friends and/or close family members. This why it's important as the bible states to renew our minds daily. In Romans 12:2, it reads *"Do not conform to the pattern of this world, but be transformed by the renewing of your mind."* It's important that we take daily inventory of our thoughts and what we are imagining. Whatever we focus on will expand.

I learned this through playing sports. I learned that through my imagination that I could change situations. As my mentor often said, your imagination can change your situations. If you are going to fulfill your purpose on this earth you must begin with your imagination. Everything that I have accomplish thus far in

My prayer for you and others is that we experience the power of God daily through the stretching of our faith and that we never become complacent with settling for a mediocre life.

ABOUT THE AUTHOR

Author, businessman and motivational speaker **Lee Green** is considered one of the best in regards to inspiring and assisting individuals in achieving their goals and dreams. Lee Green uses basketball as a platform to equip young athletes for success beyond the game. He also operates a successful youth basketball organization called **Lee Green Basketball**, which was founded in 2006. He has well over 200+ kids participating in his organization and now has programs in multiple states. The Lee Green Basketball program has helped a multitude of athletes continue their athletic careers at the collegiate and professional level.

For more information on Lee Green please visit:

www.LeeGreenBasketballAcademy.com

For speaking engagements please contact us at:

info@leegreenbasketball.com

or 214-390-6575